24 Days Until Christmas

Kristian Goldmund Aumann

Published by Kristian Goldmund Aumann, 2022.

24 DAYS UNTIL CHRISTMAS

First edition. October 8, 2022.

ISBN: 979-8215997376

Written by Kristian Goldmund Aumann.

Also by Kristian Goldmund Aumann

24 Days Until Christmas

Watch for more at www.kunstverbindetmenschen.com.

24 Days Until Christmas
24 Christmas Poems

by

KRISTIAN GOLDMUND AUMANN

"A magic came out of your smile,
Gold thread of gold thread – Stars illuminating the sky."
Kristian Goldmund Aumann

24 Days Until Christmas

POET

KRISTIAN GOLMUND AUMANN is an author, screenwriter, filmmaker, director and actor – he lives and works in St. Andrä-Wördern nearby Vienna / Austria. He has been trained at the Lee Strasberg School followed by longer-term commitment, at the Vienna Burgtheater (Claus Peymann era) and at the Italian State Theatre. Kristian has had Theatre directing and major supporting roles in TV series and films.

He has authored and published nine POETRY BOOKS in the United States, as well as numerous publications in important international poetry anthologies and magazines. He currently works on the volumne of prose named "FROM RIGHT HERE TO OVER THERE" which will be published in fall 2022. The theatrical monologue "THE NIGHTMARE of the ARTIST" was published in the German "Playwright Catalogue 2014" for State Theatre, in January 2014. The motion picture project "THE WHITE HOPE", a social critical comedy drama, is in the production phase. KRISTIAN GOLDMUND AUMANN is a member of "IG authors Authors Austria".

BIBLIOGRAPHY
From Poet's Hand
ISBN-13: 978-1456546328
Love Poems
ISBN-13: 978-1460915448
Night of A Thousand Suns
ISBN-13: 978-1463625757
Christmas Time is Here
ISBN-13: 978-1466359499
Children of the Earth
ISBN: 9781466047969
The Great Poet
Complete Poetical Works of Kristian Goldmund Aumann
ISBN-13: 9781476498119
Give Love A Chance
ISBN-13: 978-1484855188
The Seven Deadly Sins
ISBN-13: 978-1301128778
World Moving Love Quotations
ISBN-13: 978-1310786228

24 Days Until Christmas
24 Christmas Poems
by
Kristian Goldmund Aumann

FORWORD by the POET

Christmas the quietest time of the Year: 24 magical Christmas Poems shorten the wait for Christmas. *"Church bells are ringing from the golden tower – Candles light the night...You hold me captive, Snow-White sweet rejoicing in your hand. Scent from the fairy tale fir branches; Gentleness and loving smiles your star. I breathe for you the air of the winter – Magic from the sky down to earth."* 24 days and nights until Christmas; a sweet and mysterious seeming eternity.

1st of December

HAIKU

Christmas I
In the days of restless thoughts –
A bright light falls on my steps.
Like a sparkle of a thousand pearls.
An angel touched my lips.

2nd of December

Christmas Time I

A divine sound hover over there
And
the scent of millions of stars...
Silent of anticipation
grows
from gentle steps
From the eyes of children
laughing white hearts
Spruce tips glowing candles
And
miraculous healing is the night
There
where breathing pure
delicate
snowflakes on the window
Sweet Lips prayed
Hands folded
Day
and
Night
Counted
From heavenly hours
3rd of December

HAIKU

Christmas II
Silence in the time
The first snow fell in your laughter
Childlike anticipation
Christmas is in your heart

4th of December

Christmas Time II

Deep in my heart
Peaceful silence
A miracle in this night
Deep in my heart
Praise the bells
A surprise in this night
Deep in my heart
On snow-white branches
Golden rain of lights
Merry Christmas
It hovers above the heads
Angelic voices that floated through the Valley

5th of December

Christmas in Love I

An approaching step
Christmas stars above the head
My look in your angel eyes
And the snow crunches
A fragrant hug
Your breath warms my Soul
Heart beats of silver fir
And the snow crunches

6th of December

Christmas Time is Here I

Stars fall
from
the fragrant pines
An angel
knocks
on your door
Snow crystals
as graceful as a feather
Celebration of love
behind this night
Friends and foes shake hands
Candlelight
tactful
under my skin

KRISTIAN GOLDMUND AUMANN

7th of December

Christmas Time is Here II

Humming songs from heaven
Silent Night, Holy Night
A poem
from a thousand bright stars
Line by line
written in the snow
Silent Night, Holy Night
Aloof and not yet far
I stand still
Magnificent dress of winter
I stand still
Waiting in joyful hope
In the candlelight so cold
Silent Night, Holy Night
In my eyes
Tears dry so hot

KRISTIAN GOLDMUND AUMANN

8th of December

Christmas Time is Here III

Anticipation of children's eyes
It lights up
There
Where an angel hair
at the level of the staircase
&
The fire in the fireplace is in an uproar
There
Where are the candles
in the darkness of the night
&
Christmas Time
Step by step
Chimes from the steeple
Paced with heavenly joy in the snow

KRISTIAN GOLDMUND AUMANN

9th of December

Christmas Time is Here IV

Have you ever seen the spirit of Christmas?
White covered houses in the dark
From chimneys breathed silence
In rooms, decorated like heaven,
Colorful candles dance
Have you ever felt the spirit of Christmas?
Scent of angel hair
Fir branches in a bright dream
Lullabies for the soul
Light of the stars fall from the sky

Have you ever left the spirit of Christmas in your heart?
Flurry of snowflakes
Children's noses flattened on windows
Christmas, it blooms from their eyes

KRISTIAN GOLDMUND AUMANN

10th of December

Christmas I

Heavenly voices on my ears.
There
Where a blue moon –
Shadows lay on the window...
Dreamy gaze of a thousand stars.
Delicate steps in the snow
In the night,
Where a dream of the rooftops –
There was a touch of angel hair in the air.

11th of December

Christmas II

Guarded by an angel,
A magical sparkle in the snow –
As in a fairy tale
Were
Good prevails against Evil...
Maybe,
I am a magician –
On the nights where the river freezes from cold.
Icy wind of the North,
Gorgeously decorated trees on the banks.

12th of December

Christmas III

Only one step
In the promising light
There,
Where the path
Full of white flowers shimmering in the snow
Just a glance
In the sky
There,
Where the stars
Dance of the Angels
A rain of gold in the night

13th of December

Christmas IV

Playing with the harp
Smooth touch on delicate strings
From Divine hands
Snow crystals floating in the air
A beam of light falls deeply in your heart
Christmas time is dipped in gold

KRISTIAN GOLDMUND AUMANN

14th of December

Christmas V

Dressed in white
Contemplative
was
the night
I cover you with my wings
Then only
silence
I
am
your
angel
A lullaby in your ear
Sound cloud of heaven
You feel warm in the hours

15th of December

Waiting for Christmas

Watchful eyes –
The wind sweeps a touch of hope.
Snowflakes on the window.
Sleepless,
It counts the days of waiting,
From the child's mouth...
Patient
Walks with the stars.
Diamond dust from the sky –
A Sparkle in this night.

16th of December

Christmas in Love II

I have given you my heart
In the days where innocence from the clouds
So pure and hot the snow
I gave you my heart down at your feet
In the days where an angel
Mysterious
From heaven the bond of love

17th of December

Christmas in Love III

Heavenly smell
You are a child of winter
I see your spell
Flakes wrapped in white
An angel you are
Coming from the clouds
How sweet thy breath
You touch me sensually
With your wings
Blood red with love is my face

18th of December

Christmas in Love IV

In

the

night

Snowflakes trickling

Red Lips

of

the

tree

In

the

night

Two golden

Christmas stars

On

your

breasts

19th of December

Christmas III

An angel knocks on your door
Silent Night
Did you see the star?
Holy Night
Peace be with you
An angel knocks on your door
Bright lights in the branches
Holy snow falls in the days

KRISTIAN GOLDMUND AUMANN

20th of December

LOVE POEM

Christmas
On my skin
I feel your warmth
At night
When your lips whisper
I LOVE YOU
I see the Christmas star in your eyes
At night
When it snows white roses from heaven

21st of December

Christmas in Love V

Night like velvet
I am the prince on the white horse
Give me your heart
I'll show you where the ice flowers bloom
Snow crystals from your lips
Under sparkling stars
Give me your heart

22nd of December

Christmas in Love VI

In the bright light of the moon
A smile from your eyes
Sleigh ride through the valley
Chimes in the wind
In the bright light of the stars
Snowflakes on your hair
Crystal clear mountain stream flows
Sun glistening and pure
In the bright glow of the torches
Words
I
LOVE
YOU
From your mouth
Angelic songs a listening in the woods

KRISTIAN GOLDMUND AUMANN

23rd of December

Christmas in Love VII

In the evening when the moon from your eyes
I will cover you with kisses of red roses
Smell of your breath during a sleepless night
In the morning when the sun rays on your shoulders
I will cover you with kisses of white roses
Gold threads woven words on your lips

24th of December

Holy Night

CHRIST the SAVIOUR is HERE
Scent of Christmas from the valleys
There
Where the chimneys
Beaded snowflakes from the sky
Peace on earth
An incense candle rattles the cold
There
Where the pine trees
Snow on sparkling crowns
And
Hopefully bells sounded from the window arches
Wondrously light
Gold shone
Angel hair enthroned the torches there

And
Salvation throught the Saviour
Awe of the Christmas carols
There
Where the disclosure
White as snow
Deep
In the night

CHRISTMAS QUOTATIONS
by
KRISTIAN GOLDMUND AUMANN

"Christmas is a time of silent waiting."

Kristian Goldmund Aumann

"Out of the Darkness, Into the Light: The Time before Christmas is the Time of Light and mutual Love."

Kristian Goldmund Aumann

"Open your heart - stay in silence & let it
be Christmas, every day, in your life."

Kristian Goldmund Aumann

"Love is the jewel of mankind."

Kristian Goldmund Aumann

61

"Love is to feel your breath."

Kristian Goldmund Aumann

62

"On Christmas Eve a child will be born for us, a child who will give us love - that's what an angel said; and suddenly out of the darkness comes a light."

Kristian Goldmund Aumann

"Christmas; magnificent snowflakes snowing in your hope."

Kristian Goldmund Aumann

"Be filled with the spirit of christmas. Be touched by angels of love."

Kristian Goldmund Aumann

"LOVE FILL the WORLD with WONDER."

Kristian Goldmund Aumann

"Christmas; Be the Light for those who stand in the Dark."

Kristian Goldmund Aumann

"Let's open a window for Christmas."

Kristian Goldmund Auman

69

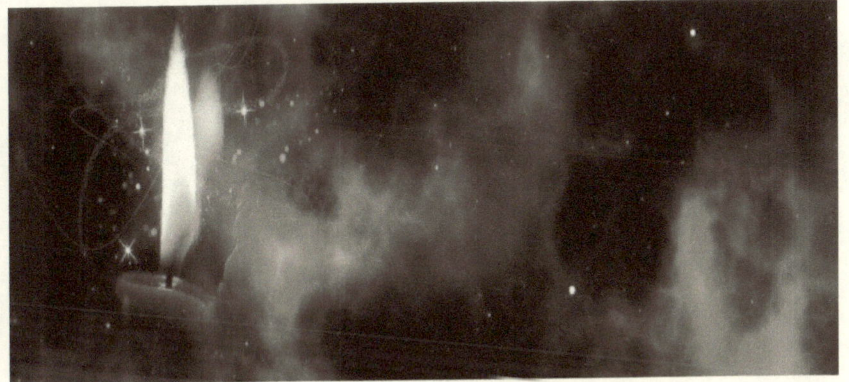

"When light comes into our hearts.
Then light comes into our dark streets."

Kristian Goldmund Aumann

Table of Contents

Don't miss out!

Visit the website below and you can sign up to receive emails whenever Kristian Goldmund Aumann publishes a new book. There's no charge and no obligation.

https://books2read.com/r/B-A-LTOT-NZVBC

BOOKS 2 READ

Connecting independent readers to independent writers.

Did you love *24 Days Until Christmas*? Then you should read *No More Wars Love & Peace is the Way*[1] by Kristian Goldmund Aumann!

[2]

War, Climate Change & Corona

In a severely tarnished world, it takes a lot of **HEALING LOVE** that must come from us. A collective shoulder "Without fear of fear" with truthfulness, respect, peacefulness, humanity, determination, justice and above all the courage to face these challenges.

50 Selected Best Famous Love Poems - Clock for Clock - Rhythm of Love beats the Clock

When love came into the world there was a magic in the air, this touching moment made our hearts beating - and amazement, she, kept our eyes open. What would be, if there was no love in the world? The

---

1. https://books2read.com/u/38ep8Z

2. https://books2read.com/u/38ep8Z

world would be convered with darkness. Therefore, let us keep the love
alive.

Also by Kristian Goldmund Aumann

24 Days Until Christmas

Watch for more at www.kunstverbindetmenschen.com.

About the Author

KRISTIAN GOLMUND AUMANN is an author, screenwriter, filmmaker, director and actor – he lives and works in St. Andrä-Wördern nearby Vienna / Austria. He has been trained at the Lee Strasberg School followed by longer-term commitment, at the Vienna Burgtheater (Claus Peymann era) and at the Italian State Theatre. Kristian has had Theatre directing and major supporting roles in TV series and films. He has authored and published nine POETRY BOOKS in the United States, as well as numerous publications in important international poetry anthologies and magazines. He currently works on the volumne of prose named "FROM RIGHT HERE TO OVER THERE" which will be published in fall 2022. The theatrical monologue "THE NIGHTMARE of the ARTIST" was published in the German "Playwright Catalogue 2014" for State Theatre, in January 2014. The motion picture project "THE WHITE HOPE", a social critical comedy drama, is in the production phase. KRISTIAN

GOLDMUND AUMANN is a member of "IG authors Authors Austria".

BIBLIOGRAPHY
From Poet's Hand
ISBN-13: 978-1456546328
Love Poems
ISBN-13: 978-1460915448
Night of A Thousand Suns
ISBN-13: 978-1463625757
Christmas Time is Here
ISBN-13: 978-1466359499
Children of the Earth
ISBN: 9781466047969
The Great Poet
Complete Poetical Works of Kristian Goldmund Aumann
ISBN-13: 9781476498119
Give Love A Chance
ISBN-13: 978-1484855188
The Seven Deadly Sins
ISBN-13: 978-1301128778
World Moving Love Quotations
ISBN-13: 978-1310786228

Read more at www.kunstverbindetmenschen.com.

www.ingramcontent.com/pod-product-compliance
Lightning Source LLC
Chambersburg PA
CBHW051251160726
47994CB00003B/1114